$\mathcal{S}till$POINT

Loss, Longing, and Our Search for God

"Regis Martin is a sage for our time. Here he offers us wisdom for confronting the greatest mystery of life: suffering and death. Yet he does so with real grace and poetic wit. Divine truth joined to the practical challenges of human life; that's what we all need, and what Martin offers in abundance. Along with profound insights, you will find encouragement and hope, coming from the God of mercy through the cross of Christ."

Scott Hahn
Author of *The Lamb's Supper*

"Regis Martin leads the reader to confront some of the great mysteries of our existence, reflecting on life and death, hope and despair, as well as the anxieties and the perplexity we feel about the unknowns to come and the unknowns with which we engage regularly. He shares concrete examples, many from his own life, but also those from great minds who explore questions which both they and we must face. All of this is done in a context of our faith."

Most Reverend John J. Myers
Archbishop of Newark

"Regis Martin has a campus-wide reputation for a remarkable vocabulary, punctuating lectures with apt quotes from poets, theologians, and the occasional rock star, and unflinchingly exploring the real problems of suffering, evil, and death. This lovely book shows his reputation is well deserved as he wrestles with deep human longings and offers us the hope of Christ: 'O death, where is your victory? O death, where is your sting?'"

Rev. Terrence Henry, T.O.R.
President
Franciscan University of Steubenville

"With the eloquence and poignancy of a poet, Regis Martin gets to the heart of life's most urgent questions, forging a link between our 'desperate desires' and our 'homesickness for God' in this profound and beautiful book."

Rev. Peter John Cameron, O.P.
Editor-in-Chief, *Magnificat*

"Regis Martin is one of Catholicism's trustworthy guides to the spiritual life in all its dimensions—including, as he demonstrates here, its hard and challenging dimensions."

George Weigel
Distinguished Senior Fellow
Ethics and Public Policy Center

"Regis Martin's moving reflection on our death-haunted and restless search for God is both beautiful and bracing. Drawing on the profound imaginings of our poets and our theologians, Martin's meditation takes place on the lip of the abyss as he shows us who it is our hearts so restlessly long for."

Gregory Erlandson
President
Our Sunday Visitor Publishing

"Regis Martin probes the deepest wounds we suffer—loss and longing—and presents us with our hope for healing: while we ache, we are 'alive with longing.' This book is as haunting and hypnotic as the poetry on which it depends. Martin applies the 'poetry of the transcendent' as a balm, the first dose in the course of a cure. You will not forget the stories he tells you. His reading of familiar biblical passages will not fail to move you and shake you."

Mike Aquilina
Author of *Why Me?: When Bad Things Happen*

"This book beautifully proclaims the Gospel in a unique and deeply poetic manner. Drawing on poetry, philosophy, theology, and the depths of human experience, Regis Martin lyrically connects the deepest longings and hopes of the human heart with their overwhelmingly generous fulfillment in Christ. This book can only increase our own desperate desire for eternal love and fulfillment and deepen our hope in its certain coming to pass."

Ralph Martin
Director of Graduate Theology Programs in the New Evangelization
Sacred Heart Major Seminary

"Regis Martin is a masterful writer who, with wit and charm, draws the reader into a dialogue with some of the greatest thinkers and writers of human history—to ask the questions that lie deep within each person's heart. This is a breathtakingly beautiful book that will stir within any reader a longing to deepen their personal relationship with the Person of Jesus Christ."

Mike Sullivan
President
Catholics United for the Faith

"Regis Martin not only knows and loves the truth, he expounds upon it beautifully. *Still Point* is a captivating look at the most perplexing and unavoidable aspects of life's voyage. Overwhelmed by desperate desires, which appear to go unnoticed, and then unsatisfied, we are led to see that, in the end, love will find a way."

Curtis Martin
President and Founder
Fellowship of Catholic University Students

$\mathcal{S}till$POINT

Loss, Longing, and Our Search for God

Regis Martin

ave maria press AMP notre dame, indiana

Founded in 1865, Ave Maria Press is a ministry of the United States Province of Holy Cross.

www.avemariapress.com

Paperback: ISBN-10 1-59471-341-3   ISBN-13 978-1-59471-341-5

E-book: ISBN-10 1-59471-358-8   ISBN-13 978-1-59471-358-3

Cover image © Don Paulson Photography/Purestock/SuperStock.

Cover and text design by Andy Wagoner.

Printed and bound in the United States of America.

Library of Congress Cataloging-in-Publication Data

Martin, Regis, 1946-

　Still point : loss, longing, and our search for God / Regis Martin.

　　p. cm.

　ISBN 978-1-59471-341-5 (pbk.) -- ISBN 1-59471-341-3 (pbk.)

　1.　Hope--Religious aspects--Catholic Church.　I. Title.

BV4638.M385 2012

234'.25--dc23

2012022134

In memory of my father . . .

Regis E. Martin Sr.

1919–2011

"Is it the gods who put this fire in our minds, or is it that each man's relentless longing becomes a god to him?"
Virgil, *Aeneid*

"The very existence of the question implies the existence of an answer."
Luigi Giussani, *The Religious Sense*

"Where is God? Where is God now?"
Elie Wiesel, *Night*

"At the still point of the turning world."
T. S. Eliot, *Four Quartets*

CONTENTS

The state of being lost—what does it mean? We all want to go home: J. Cheever vignette. The fear of death and the dread of what may come after. M. Unamuno and *the tragic sense of life*. Finding the *still point*, and thus God, in the midst of desolation and death. Introducing the theme of hope and the argument of the book.

Chapter 1

A mother's death . . . an unread book . . . the Holocaust of the Jews . . . the strangled cry from the Cross . . . the Mystery of Holy Saturday. What do these have in common? Establishing the truth that God is love: "*the strongest argument of all*" (JPII). God's radical solidarity in a world too often resistant to his Suffering Servant.

Chapter 2

How to cross an infinite sea on a finite bridge: C. S. Lewis and *A Grief Observed*. What if God does not want us after all? The bastion of hope and those who assault it: J. Didion and *The Year of Magical Thinking*. Aquinas, Eros, and the human longing to see the beloved. The horror of an everlasting nonfulfillment.

Chapter 3

Going in search of the lost: the lesson of Orpheus and Eurydice. What do we really want? The ground of desire and the anguish of never getting it. The answer is eschatology. Canvassing the mystery of the End and the need for hope. Peguy's "tiny girl," who gets up each morning. "Everything is grace" (St. Thérèse).

Chapter 4

The fate of those untouched by tremors of an ultimate bliss. How different the stand of the Christian in relation to the End! Nihilism and Richard Rorty. The "terrible sonnets" of Gerard Manley Hopkins. And what if God himself were not to be found on the other side? The witness of Alfred Delp. Introducing the subjunctive.

Chapter 5

Once more, the sheer thrust of human longing. Richard Wilbur's "The House." Why is it never hopeless to hope? The analysis of Lewis; the judgment of Aquinas. Weighting the hydraulics of hope: G. Marcel and "the ontological mystery." Love augments hope: "Thou shalt not die!" Seeing prayer as its voice.

Chapter 6

Lost and found: the experience of little Luigi (Giussani). Life understood as search. Finding the formula for the journey. Dante and Tom Hanks: the sense of being a castaway. The true protagonist of history—the beggar. The knight's quest at the heart of *The Seventh Seal*. To be rescued by Christ: "I did not know my longing, till I encountered You."

Chapter 7

The high school years I never remembered, save for a single event I have never forgotten. An image of death linking two extraordinary lives and what it means. Seeing the skull beneath the skin in the face of a dead relative. Images in Webster and Shakespeare. Death and hell: the two supreme evils, from which Christ has freed us. Hopkins's masterful poem as concluding illustration of the point.

Chapter 8

Assessing the cynic's dismissal: how can a mere mood vanquish death? Examples of life's seeming triumph: Camus, Alice Walker, and Bishop Henry King. The refusal of stoic resignation: Edna St. Vincent Millay's quiet gesture of protest. The world of pagan pessimism and why "No hay remedio" is not an option. Father Murray's *Problem of God* and why the God hypothesis alone satisfies.

My brother's illness and death. The Church that would not turn her back on him. A single imperishable memory and how the meaning of it changed my life. Arrested by Rilke's "Autumn." A final resolution to the tensions of gravity and grace, death and life. Thanks be to Christ—who "plays in ten thousand places"—we know the story's outcome, and it is good.

INTRODUCTION

When I first began this little book, a window of opportunity having suddenly opened to allow me to write it, I kept hearing this phrase, *desperate desire*, going off like a firecracker in my head. And while I could never quite trace its precise origin, it seemed to me so telling a phrase that I seized upon it at once, determined to use it as both theme and title for the book. Alas, I had not reckoned with the warhead I was proposing to launch. (A brief Google search would soon reveal the full if unwitting extent of my folly.) Wiser counsels thereupon prevailed, with the happy result that a very different and, I have no doubt, less provocative title was then chosen—concerning which I will have something to say a little later on. . . .

Still, the idea behind the phrase, *desperate desire*, has stayed with me. The theme survived, you might say, the title's suppression. For as long as I can remember, in fact, its meaning has remained fixed in my mind. Indeed, the awful resonance of the thing continues to haunt my memory. It all began when, as a small child lost in a park following a family picnic, I wandered disconsolately about in an ever more frantic, desperate search for my parents. Yet my predicament was hardly hopeless. My family, after all, having at once realized I'd gone missing, mobilized straightaway their return to the park in order to fetch me. So it was, in retrospect, the briefest of separations. Besides, a kind contingent of campers, seeing me stumbling about in tears, quickly gathered me up and, between popsicles designed to assuage my grief, they drove me home.

Nevertheless, not knowing that a rescue mission was on its way, how could I possibly imagine the shape, much less the speed, it would take? And isn't that the whole point about being lost? *That the child simply cannot know.* And, of course, when it comes to being lost, we are all children. In her moving account of the short-story writer John Cheever, his daughter Susan explains the origin of her book's title *Home*

Before Dark: "My father liked to tell a story about my younger brother Fred," she begins about her brother who, at the end of a long summer's day, espied their father,

> standing outside the house under the big elm tree that shaded the flagstones in front of the door. . . . And when he saw Daddy standing there he ran across the grass and threw his little boy's body into his father's arms.
>
> "I want to go home, Daddy," he said, "I want to go home." Of course he *was* home, just a few feet from the front door, in fact. But that didn't make any difference, as my father well understood. We all want to go home, he would say when he told this story. We all do.

But what if there were no home to go to, no one to welcome the child when he got there, indeed, his own father telling him in words so final that nothing more could ever be said to soften the sentence: "I do not know you"? Would that not force one out into a state of aloneness, solitude, and sorrow that, in point of fact, none of us was created to have to endure?

Let me say it again. What if there really were a loneliness so final that nothing in this world could remedy the pain of it? A circumstance of abandonment so definitive that neither word nor gesture could deliver us from it? Would not that frightful condition find its precise and formal theological equivalent in what we call hell? Isn't hell that very depth of loneliness where no love, no relation of real communion, can reach one in order to set free the soul of one's solitude? A life bereft of both hope and home, lacking all sense of community, or sanctuary, or escape? Think of the prodigal son fated never to find his father's love but, like the Flying Dutchman, is left aimless and alone forever—an eternity of grief, no less. Who could bear it?

Isn't that what makes us most afraid of death? That the inevitable darkness awaiting us is perhaps but a prelude to still greater horrors? Asked once by an interviewer what bothered him most about life, the poet Robert Lowell answered simply, "That people die." And knowing nothing of what may lie on the other side (Shakespeare's "undiscovered country" is not a place from which we are free to return), the mind naturally falls prey to the most awful phantoms of fear and desolation. Death, you see, is never far away; the beast is always close at hand. And wherever it is he lurks, even were he to hide behind the nearest shrub, his jaws are poised ever to strike the unsuspecting. No one gets out alive. There is no gainsaying the Old Guy—nor, as I say, the dread of what may come after. Hidden in the shadows, he remains always at the ready, always set to pounce. "It is the blight man was born for," says the narrator of Gerard Manley Hopkins's *Spring and Fall* to the young child who has wandered innocently into the autumn woods where, weeping but not knowing why, she watches all the fallen leaves die. "Margaret," he asks, "are you grieving / Over Goldengrove unleaving?" And with what has always struck me as a kind of brutal finality, he tells her, "It is Margaret you mourn for."

We must all die, and so, like young Margaret, we are given over to grief at the loss even of the leaves, since in nature's passing we glimpse the clearest prefiguring of our own. But have you noticed? We are not resigned to die—neither are we resigned to suffer, or to remain always alone—and so we rage (most of us, I suspect) "against the dying of the light." It is not only poets, I am saying, who exhort us to resist going "gentle into that good night," to recall the moving words so sternly spoken by the

Welsh poet Dylan Thomas to his own father as he teeters on the cliff edge of death. The life force itself is quite sufficient to move humankind to "burn and rave at close of day." These things are a problem for us, an outrage even, against the heart of what it means to be human, which is the yearning to live always, and in communion with others, and without pain.

Is the problem even soluble? Or is it instead one of those intractable things the unraveling of which meets head on with *mystery* itself, which is a wall too massive for mere reason to knock down? The problem is the very thing, in other words, we feel obliged to try to penetrate yet remain powerless to do so. ("Human reason has this peculiar fate," reports Immanuel Kant in his *Critique of Pure Reason*, "that . . . it is burdened by questions which . . . it is not able to ignore, but which, as transcending all its powers, it is also not able to answer.") In short, the mind is forced to look elsewhere, to lift its sights still higher. "Leaving one still," to quote a telling passage from T. S. Eliot's *Four Quartets*, "with the intolerable wrestle with words and meanings." And so, like the figure of Jacob locked in mortal struggle with the angel, we dare not desist until we too have extracted a blessing. There can be no rest, I am saying, no quitting the field, until one arrives at real and lasting resolution, a resolution, moreover, that refusing any sort of cheap and facile closure, reaches right into the very heart of the human condition, which is one of forlorn brokenness beneath an immense weight of sin, suffering, and death. It must do justice, in other words, to that *tragic sense of life* that Miguel de Unamuno among others rightly insists is the chief, aboriginal truth about man. "The man of flesh and bone; the man who is born, suffers, and dies—above all, who dies." Not the talking head, not the mere idea of man, his mind filled with the empty straw of abstractions that know nothing of passion or pain. It was not the concept of humankind that engaged Unamuno, who could never put his trust either in the adjective "human" or the substantive "humanity," both of which he fiercely and categorically rejected as no better than a pair of bloodless abstractions untethered to the world he knew, which was always a real and concrete place, circumscribed by the exigencies of time and circumstance, sin and sorrow. Only someone who actually does exist, he would repeatedly insist, is qualified to speak, because only he is "infinitely interested in existing."

Moved by considerations of this sort, what I aim
to do here is to set down a few modest reflections
regarding this business of living in a world that—
given the sheer frightful insolubility of its problems,
chief of which being suffering and death—one quite
understandably desires, and most desperately so, to
escape. From what do we wish to escape? We desire
to escape from the very terms of death and desolation
that life imposes. And to what end? Where are we to
escape to? To the *still point*. And why is that? Because
it is necessary to do so in order to anchor the soul to
that which finally transcends death, desolation, and
loss—and thus to fulfill that longing for God that is
both constitutive of who we are and indispensible to
what we hope to become. The maintenance of our
human dignity, you could say, the very life of the
soul, depends on holding fast to the *still point*. Without God, we are less than zero; indeed, we become
a kind of demonic nothingness. Honorable escape,
therefore, is an urgent need of the human heart. We
simply must try and find a way past the sheer desolation of death, those "vasty halls of death" of which
the poet Matthew Arnold speaks, whose lethal coils
have wrapped themselves tightly round our lives. We
need to navigate our way past that fearsome, devour-
ing figure, the awful dragon about whom St. Cyril

of Jerusalem warned the catechumens of the early Church who had come to him for instruction: "The dragon is by the side of the road," he told them, "watching those who pass. Beware lest he devour you. We go the father of souls, but it is necessary to pass by the dragon."

None of this can happen, of course, without attention being paid to the *still point*, to the sheer mystery of that time and place where, says T. S. Eliot, "past and future are gathered." It is the point on which all the polarities converge—matter and meaning, grit and grace, history and heaven, man and God. "Except for the point," he reminds us, "the still point, / There would be no dance, and there is only the dance." Here is the point toward which the poetry of *Four Quartets*, Eliot's enduring masterpiece, moves in its own rhythmic, sublime dance.

How we all long for this union; it is the consummation we most devoutly, most deeply, desire.

> The inner freedom from the
>   practical desire,
> The release from action and
>   suffering, release from the inner

> And the outer compulsion, yet
>   surrounded
> By a grace of sense, a white light
>   still and moving.

To rivet one's gaze, one's entire life even, upon this—thus always, as Eliot says, "to apprehend / The point of intersection of the timeless / With time, is an occupation for the saint." Here, of course, as we know perfectly well, and Eliot is not shy in saying so, is a finality toward which we do not move very well, nor often, nor quickly. Nevertheless, as Eliot himself predicts with uncanny Augustinian accuracy, "For most of us this is the aim / Never here to be realised; / Who are only undefeated / Because we have gone on trying."

How wonderfully, how stubbornly, too, we persist in this desire! In fact, as I will argue in the book, the very existence of this desire, when pushed especially to the point of desperation, provides real testimony, albeit oblique and paradoxical, to that adamantine quality of hope on which, finally, our conquest of death does depend. "Tell all the truth," in other words, "but tell it slant," to quote that most enigmatic of American poets, Emily Dickinson:

Success in Circuit lies
Too bright for our infirm Delight
The Truth's superb surprise.

In doing so, I submit, such testimony furnishes a way of shoring up the argument for the existence of a good and gracious God, who alone is able to put all our fears to flight.

What will it take, I am asking, what precisely is required, in order for each of us to be able to say in the teeth of all the pain, travail, and sadness that encircle our lives—including most especially the threat of death and that dread of something worse to follow—that none of this will finally matter? When will we be able to say, illumined by hope, that when we walk through the valley of the shadow of death, it will not have been a mere whistling in the dark, because, in fact, the world really has been flooded with light, a light of such radiant, indestructible incandescence that the darkness simply cannot overmaster it? Thanks be to Christ, then, for having come among us to suffer and to die, because it is only on the strength of his person, and the trail he sets himself to blaze, that we may find ourselves free at last to declare, *"Death . . . thou shalt die!"*

CHAPTER ❶

When my mother died, following a sudden and massive heart attack in September 1995, our family fell into a state of profound, protracted grief. Because it was so entirely unexpected, the news was received with incomprehension. The signs were certainly there all right, but no one had noticed. In hindsight, I now see that my brother Kevin's death two years before from AIDS may well have hastened her own end. The suffering of her youngest child, the one she had agonized over the most, caused her unspeakable distress.

By an odd coincidence, earlier that day I had been sent an advance copy of my first book, *The Suffering of Love: Christ's Descent Into the Hell of Human*

Hopelessness, which she had looked forward to with pleasure. Based on a dissertation I had done in Rome where I had been a student at the Angelicum during the years 1984 to 1988, it attempted to answer a question that has tormented not a few anguished souls, most especially those who had fallen victim to the genocidal passions of Adolph Hitler and the Nazi machinery of hatred and revenge he had unleashed. Here, unmistakably, was the cry of God's People, the Chosen of Israel, the People of the Book, to whom all the promises of God had first been given. And amid the death camps of the Third Reich, the full-throated cry of European Jewry went unheard, unheeded. Where was God? What was he doing while the engines of extermination were being carefully stoked by Hitler and his evil empire? Did God not care that six million of his people were going up in smoke? Why were the architects of the Final Solution seemingly given a free pass? Indeed, where is God to be found in the midst of so many other nameless horrors that mark the long, dark journey of human history?

Where else would God be found—I would argue—if not on the side of those who suffer? The strangled cry from the Cross—"My God, my God, why hast thou forsaken me?"—seemed to me evidence enough of God's solidarity with suffering humanity. In pitching his tent in our midst, did he not show himself in a way sufficient to encompass the entire universe? In the image of the disfigured Christ so eloquently depicted by the artist Mathias Grünewald, for instance, the entire body of our Savior is covered over with boils, mute testimony to the torments of countless plague victims for whom, surely, no closer identification with God's Suffering Servant could possibly exist.

What more—I asked myself—does the world require? Isn't this convicting enough to establish the claims made by Christ? What further proof do we need that he is the world's salvation? And does it not also vacate every objection, every insult hurled, against God? Lay before God every injustice ever inflicted upon the innocent; heap high the pile of accumulated miseries so that it rises as high as heaven itself; and the sheer goodness of God will triumphantly survive over every possible iniquity and travail borne by humankind. The purity of the sacrifice of God's love for the world will overcome even the obscenity of the Holocaust. In the face of a spectacle so sacredly terrifying as the sight of the living God himself stretched out upon the Cross—slowly tortured to death by men determined on maximizing his pain and ignominy—who would not wish for consolation from one who had come among us to suffer and to die?

In his searing account of the death of the "sad-eyed angel," whose story lies at the heart of *Night*, arguably the darkest and most despairing memoir to emerge from the experience of the Holocaust, Elie Wiesel reveals an extremity of evil so great, so all-encompassing (we are told), that it can never fully be understood by us, nor redeemed by God. For reasons horrifyingly capricious, a young boy has been singled out by the Gestapo to die by hanging, all the inmates of the camp meanwhile having been conscripted to watch. And as he dangles horribly in front of everyone, Wiesel hears a man call out, "Where is God? Where is God now?" When the grisly business is at last at an end, the prisoners are forced to file by the corpse. Once more, Wiesel hears the plaintive cry asking where is God in the midst of so unspeakable a horror. Only now, however, he hears himself answer in a whisper that none can overhear: "Here he is, here is God."

Wiesel's point, which plainly edges the reader in the direction of a total eclipse of hope, is that both God and the little boy died at the end of that rope, perishing together in the death camps of the Third Reich. Only Hitler kept his promises to the Jews, not God. Yet, if the fate of God and the Jew really are tied to the same noose, then here at last is the most arresting evidence we'll ever have of the sheer radicality of divine love. How could God provide more graphic proof of his compassionate regard for the world than to show us his pierced and crucified Son hanging on a cross? How else could he love us "to the end" if not by revealing the very wounds of love? Do we really require yet more evidence from God in order for him to comfort the innocent, the oppressed? He "emptied himself, taking the form of a servant, being born in the likeness of men . . . became obedient unto death, even death on a cross" (Phil 2:7–8).

Here, insists Blessed John Paul II in a profound reflection from his book *Crossing the Threshold of Hope*, is "*the strongest argument*. If the agony on the Cross had not happened, the truth that God is Love would have been unfounded."

And, yes, there is more. Christ's *kenosis* continues, deepens even, until, finally, reaching into the shame and the silence of Holy Saturday, he undergoes an extremity of such loss as to appear absolute and eternal. Christ goes, in a word, to hell—to commune with the spirits of the dead, whose separation from God, from every communication with the living, leaves them in a state of seeming dereliction and abandonment forever. These spirits are cut off, it would appear, from the springs of joy and hope in an absolute and definitive way. Ah, but the design of this Descent, so singular and paradoxical in its rhythm, will instead bring the world salvation! Jesus will later assure the Lady Julian of Norwich in a series of shattering revelations vouchsafed to this extraordinary English lay woman of the fourteenth century: "As I have made good the greatest damages, so I intend that you understand from this that I will make good all that is defective." What kind of a God could get away with saying something like that, a promise so palpably extravagant, so sublimely over the top? "That all shall be well and all manner of thing shall be well." Who can believe it? And at such a frightful cost to Christ, we can scarcely credit it. Pope Benedict XVI has observed, "It is the day which expresses the unparalleled experience of our age, anticipating the fact that God is simply absent, that the grave hides him, that he no longer speaks, so that one no longer needs to gainsay him but can simply overlook him."

In his very absence, in the mode of concealment and disguise God chose in sending his Son to suffer and die for humankind, God hit upon a strategy of descent no more daring and dramatic than can be imagined. By contriving so complete and headlong a plunge into the heart of eternal darkness (all that I had in fact sought to set forth in the dissertation), Christ succeeds in so overcoming the forces of evil that, in the person of the "strong man" whom he wrestles to the ground and subdues, the great *harrowing of hell* takes place, thus freeing humans from the power of death—a power none of us could ever have vanquished on our own.

Hans Urs von Balthasar, in a passage from his sermon "Bought at a Great Price" on the theme of the cost borne by the Son of God to obtain our salvation, notes that, for large numbers of people,

> it is simply up to them to reconcile themselves with God, and that many do not need such reconciliation at all. . . . They have no conception of the flames necessary to burn up all the refuse that is within man; they have no idea that

these flames burn white hot in the Cross of Jesus. There is a cry that penetrates all the cool pharisaism of our alleged religiosity: "My God, my God, why have you forsaken me?" In the darkest night of the soul, while every fiber of his body is in pain, and he experiences extreme thirst for God, for lost love, he atones for our comfortable indifference.

It was precisely because Christ wished to pay the highest possible price for our salvation that he mounted the Cross on Golgotha. "Not only has he *canceled* our huge debt," Balthasar reminds us, which is what the master in the New Testament parable did for his servant, "for it is not simply a matter of money that we cannot pay: he has *borne* our guilt or given *himself* for us as our 'ransom.' For the point is that we cannot free *ourselves* from our alienation from God."

But does anyone really believe this anymore? How credible is the Christian claim for those who live thoroughly secularized lives—people whose worldly horizons have been swept clean of all dogmatic dust? It has been observed that in order to really know what people believe, it is necessary to know of what they are afraid. Certainly for the Christian annealed to the Cross of Jesus Christ, the truly awful fear is that, notwithstanding the sacrifice made by Christ, it will not matter one whit to the world, because, in its blithe and bourgeois way, it simply does not regard itself as requiring any sort of redemption at all, much less the blood-spattered body of a dead God. For such as these (that is, people unwilling to take ownership even of their own sins), it will be necessary to show, to demonstrate in the clearest and most graphic way, the extent of their alienation from God, indeed, to plumb the very depth of their denial of God, before the proposal of faith is likely to take root. Why call the physician if you think yourself perfectly fit? C. S. Lewis writes in the essay "God in the Dock" that first appeared back in 1948, "The greatest barrier I have met is the almost total absence from the minds of my audience of any sense of sin." And yet it is in the very nature of the revelation that Christ himself came to enflesh, adducing its most perfect monstration in his broken body upon the Cross, that merely to look upon the crucified God is to begin to understand that what passes for human love is often nothing more than a front for the sheer egoism of the self-centered self. We say no as often as the Son of Man says yes. And so we must start from the very beginning with Christ, back to bedrock, if we wish to learn what it means to suffer and to serve.

That, at any rate, was the design of the dissertation I'd written, the burden of the book I'd hoped my mother would live to read.

CHAPTER ❷

A couple of other things happened around the period of my mother's death that remain fixed in the memory of that sad time. For one thing, our daughter Elizabeth was about to be born, whom we would name after her; she would, in the years since her passing, grow most uncannily to resemble the lovely woman she never knew.

Did I say *never* knew, that she had never known my mother? Because during the years of her childhood, and also those of her two younger siblings, each was endearingly under the illusion that he or she must have clearly known my mother, having obviously seen her in heaven, which is where they were before getting their bodies for the journey into the material world. It took a good deal of theological huffing and puffing, let me tell you, to blow that house of straw down. The thought of heaven as some vast lumber-yard where souls, like so many planks of wood waiting to be sold, is not the sort of childhood conceit of which one can easily disabuse the very young. Our youngest continues to remain resistant to the idea of bodies and souls beginning life together.

The other thing going on, of course, was the O. J. Simpson trial, then nearing its noisome end. What an odious business that was. Yet another anodyne amid an endless stream (the media circus surrounding the death of Princess Di and the sex life of William Jefferson Clinton were not far off), leaving us, in the language of T. S. Eliot's *Four Quartets*, "Distracted from distraction by distraction." I remember telling someone at the time, "Oh, well, at least my mother now knows if he really did it or not." So, too, as regards the book she never saw: knowing its thesis from a higher vantage point, she need hardly have read it.

But hold on a minute. Do I, in point of fact, really know any of this to be true? Does anyone know? The distance between us, the gap separating the living from the dead, limns an infinite and absolute sea of being, across which there are simply no engineering skills for throwing a bridge. And even if it were possible to go there, like the mythic Orpheus in search of Eurydice amid the shades of the underworld, what guarantee do I have that she is there? That anyone is there?

In *A Grief Observed*, C. S. Lewis's heartbreaking account of his wife's death, her sudden felt absence from his life proved so searing that he could only publish it under a pseudonym, so painfully did he experience the loss. And to well-meaning souls who sought ways of escape for him, he found it difficult to be forbearing.

> It is hard to have patience with people who say, "There is no death" or "Death doesn't matter." There is death. And whatever is matters. . . . You might as well say that birth doesn't matter. I look up at the night sky. Is anything more certain that in all those vast times and spaces, if I were allowed to search them, I should nowhere find her face, her voice, her touch? She died. She is dead. Is the word so difficult to learn?

No, it is not. But while it is hardly a stretch having to learn the word, or even to accept the fact that those we love must die, it is surely something else again being told to acquiesce in never seeing them again, indeed, of not even finding oneself on the other side. Here is fear enough to harrow the heart of anyone. It plainly tormented even so robust an apologist as Lewis, whom we justly celebrate for the copious and eloquent overflow of his writings in defense of the basic teachings of the Christian religion, including especially the doctrine of the Resurrection. Would he—Lewis himself wondered—be told by the God for whom he'd harnessed all his literary powers, and most resolutely given over his life, that he really wasn't wanted after all? Would God leave his soul bereft at the last? Would the Lord of the Universe, in averting his gaze, abandon him to the netherworld, prey to an ultimate "horror," as he called it, "of nonentity, of annihilation"?

In that magnificent fantasy of his called *The Great Divorce*, consisting of an imaginary bus trip from hell to the outer suburbs of heaven (intended, we later learn, for day trippers who, if they wish, may stay on forever, blazing their trail of glory straight into the heart of God), the narrator, who is Lewis himself, muses most fearfully on a line of poetry from William Cowper, who, "dreaming that he was not after all doomed to perdition, at once knew the dream to be false and said, 'These are the sharpest arrows in His quiver.'" Dear God, if this is the fate that awaits those who honestly strive to please you, who spend their lives promoting the truths of the religion you sent your own Son into the world to reveal, indeed, to suffer and die for, what is to become of the rest of us?

Should we perhaps call this a major crisis of faith? Or is it rather, to speak more accurately, the bastion of hope that is under siege? How common, I wonder, are the symptoms? Certainly, they are not common among the literati of this world, for whom issues of ultimacy seem not to figure at all in their workaday calculations. The solvent of secularism, like those acids of modernity of which Karl Marx spoke when predicting how "everything solid melts into thin air," tends to inoculate such people against having to think about the next world, thus flattening out their desires for exclusively worldly ones. I am thinking, for instance, of the acclaimed author and novelist Joan Didion, whose bestselling memoir on the death of her husband, *The Year of Magical*

Thinking (a work so lionized in fashionable literary circles that some have called it the sort of book one frankly cannot die without having first read), comes down pretty emphatically on the point that, despite their having both been baptized and confirmed in the Christian faith, neither she nor her husband believed a word of it. Yet, in the midst of her grieving for the husband who is no more, Ms. Didion will nevertheless confess that, while "I did not believe in the resurrection of the body . . . I still believed that given the right circumstances he would come back."

This is an astonishing admission, the sheer incoherence of which quite takes one's breath away. By chucking the miracle of resurrection, she somehow gets her dead husband back? One would have thought, on logical grounds alone, that without the resurrection, none of us comes back. But, of course, people of her persuasion, that is, those who disavow the whole deposit of Christian hope, appear not even to miss it; so little do they mind the prospect of annihilation, of final entropy, they actually go out of their way to advertise the blessings of everlasting extinction. To dismantle the structures of human hope, and thus to level the longings of the heart, assumes programmatic shape in their lives and work. And yet, for all that they invest of themselves in squaring that particular circle, it really is an entirely perverse position for any sentient being to take, inasmuch as the desire not to remain dead forever is, well, so natural, so perfectly congruent with the most elemental disposition of humans, which is to persist always in being. After all, Eros, the life force, is the deepest urge we possess (or, to be more precise, that possesses us), the sheer surge and thrust of which awakens, in Gerard Manley Hopkins's lovely line, "the dearest freshness deep down things."

This is all, by the way, standard Catholic teaching, given superb and comprehensive expression in the thought of the Common Doctor, St. Thomas Aquinas, who, anticipating the atheist objection of our own day that says the tendency of beings born of nothingness is to return to nothingness, flat out denies that a mere orientation toward nothingness could possibly constitute the natural movement of the creature God made, since that movement can only be directed toward a good, and the good implies existence. In other words, just as all contingent reality has its source in nothingness, and humans are contingent, so too could we collapse back into nothingness, *if it were God's will*. But, says Thomas, now citing the authority of holy scripture, "He created all things that they might exist" (Wis 1:14).

How is it, then, that so many nowadays seem not the least bit nostalgic for the springs of hope, for the consolations of traditional religion? Is our longing for immortality so easily effaced? Has the level of human interest in eternity diminished that sharply since the time of our ancestors? Must we now therefore treat our thirst for streams of living water as nothing more than atavism, a sort of vestigial twitch we'll sooner or later learn to stop scratching?

Whatever longings there are in Ms. Didion's memoir, and it is heavy with the sense of loss and regret, the point is that hers is a cry of the heart not even remotely in the same ballpark as the fear and terror that evidently seized men like Cowper and Lewis. In fact, in the year following her husband's death, Joan Didion appears to have come serenely to terms with her loss, willing at last to let him go. "I know why we try to keep the dead alive," she tells us at the very end of *The Year of Magical Thinking*. It is because we want to keep them with us. Ah, but we must all grow up, and so we realize "that if we are to live ourselves there comes a point at which we must relinquish the dead, let them go, keep them dead. Let them become the photograph on the table."

Is that an acceptable alternative? I am certainly not resigned to relegating those I love to the proportions of a photographic study. What awful violence must Joan Didion have needed to self-inflict in order for her to find closure following her husband's death by relegating him to a photo album? If love means anything it means a heart so pierced and stricken when the beloved dies that nothing less than total resurrection is required to restore the blessed presence that was lost. Isn't the hope of resurrection the real solvent here? That, in a word—the longing to see the beloved once more, and forever—is not unnatural. And that the soul transfixed by the love of God is not irrational, because of a lively conviction that, in believing this, it may fasten all its desire upon the quest to obtain it.

Here is what real terror means to me—that in looking for the last time upon the face of my dead mother in the open casket, whispering a final goodbye to this remarkable woman who gave me life and nurture, the one absolute certainty I should have, for which all the evidence of science and experience combine to make real in my mind, is that I shall never see her again. If that were so, and this lifeless thing on a steel slab were never again to rise and walk, then life for me would be such a horror and an obscenity that I should scarcely wish to go on living. What would I not give to know, really to know, that in fact the dead do not stay dead but that, given the economy of the next world, they become incandescently alive in the arms of God? Like the poet Alfred Tennyson, I too should feel moved to exclaim in tones of ringing, desperate desire,

> Ah Christ, that it were possible
> For one short hour to see
> The souls we loved, that they might
>   tell us
> What and where they be.

CHAPTER ❸

I remember being greatly struck, years ago, on hearing the story of Orpheus and Eurydice for the first time. What awful, heartrending pathos surrounds this timeless and universal tale of longing and loss. A desperate man ventures bravely into the pit of hell in search of the woman he loves. Entirely untrue, of course, yet the version that has come down to us from the two great Roman poets, Virgil and Ovid, lends it a verisimilitude that seems to render the experience as real and immediate as if it had been lifted from the pages of this morning's newspaper.

We are told that, among the earliest musicians, the most gifted were the gods, chief of which was Apollo, whose music was so melodious that when all the other gods listened they could think of little else save the sweet loveliness of the sound. They even managed, for a time at least, to set aside their frequent quarrels and vendettas with one another. In fact, so tranquilizing were the tunes played by Apollo that relations between the gods and men improved as well; the killing fields would fall silent, and the gods, abandoning their predatory habits, would actually leave us alone.

Among the mortals, however, none could play as well as Orpheus, who seems to have been endowed with sublime gifts. Even the course of a river, we are told, would happily change its direction thanks to the spell cast by the magic of his lyre. And, of course, when Orpheus fell in love with Eurydice, he won her heart by the beauty of his music. But the marriage did not survive, fate having stepped in to kill her on the very day of her wedding, leaving poor Orpheus inconsolable. And because he could not bear to lose her, he resolved to follow her down into the underworld, there to retrieve his lost bride and bring her back to the land of the living. He quite succeeded in doing this, so beguiling were the sounds he emitted; indeed, it is recorded, "He drew iron tears down

Pluto's cheek, / and made Hell itself grant what Love did seek."

There was one condition, however: he must never look back at Eurydice as they climb their way together out into the upper world. Alas, the provision proves impossible for Orpheus to keep. On reaching daylight, he instinctively turns round to make certain she is still there, at which point fate again intervenes, sending her ineluctably and forever back into hell.

And although her final word is "Farewell," spoken scarcely above a whisper to the man who risked everything to save her, Orpheus is not reconciled to the loss. Indeed, his desire grown desperate, he appeals once more to the gods for permission to reenter hell, but they refuse. And so Orpheus will spend the rest of his short life wandering in desolation about the world, shunning the company of other men until, at last, a band of robbers fall upon him and tear him to pieces.

This tale is not likely to become the pilot for a new TV series, is it? If what somebody once said about the average American is ture, that what he or she most wants in entertainment is a tragedy with a happy ending, then there is simply no way to salvage even a scintilla of happiness from this story.

Leaving the realm of legend behind us, suppose we turn to a true story, this taken from the annals of a modern psychiatric study, and watch the levels of desperation rise and spill over. We are asked to imagine a large room filled with strangers—attractive strangers, all perfectly stylish and sophisticated, with neither a nerd nor a loser in the lot. Now observe them as they pair off with a partner, someone equally chic and successful, to whom they are to ask, again and again, one single question. What do you want? What do you *really* want?

What could possibly be simpler? A question so utterly innocent, you would think, that the exercise could hardly threaten a titmouse. Yet, within minutes, the room is convulsed with emotion so raw that people cannot bear the pain of weeping for all that they have lost. And so they cry out to those who are gone, those never to be seen again—so many missing mothers and fathers, wives, husbands, children, and friends. It is like an image of the dead taken from T. S. Eliot's *Wasteland*, moving in silent procession across London Bridge—"so many," he says, "I had not thought death had undone so many." Our loved ones are taken, like dead leaves fallen from the sky, carried off and burned when they die. Who can bear it? Is it not to force a human being out into an extremity of loneliness and loss so great that one would think it impossible to have to go on living? Who would not prefer annihilation to an anguish so awful that it will never end?

Yes, but suppose there were no other choice save that of having to soldier on, to brace the moral constitution to endure the unendurable? Does the Church have anything to say about this? Has it any light to throw upon this terrible longing we have to see once again those we have loved and lost; that even amid the fear and the terror of an everlasting night, there might still be hope; that it still springs eternal; and that even for Orpheus and Eurydice there is hope?

The answer, very clearly, is yes. Blazingly set forth in the Church's doctrine of the Last Things—that is, eschatology, a word that comes from the Greek word *eschata*, meaning "outcomes" or "ends"—it represents the very content of her hope, her distilled wisdom concerning the Last Things we are destined to face: the certainty of death and judgment, followed by an eternity of either heaven or hell. Here are the mysteries that impinge most directly upon the final section of the creed: "the resurrection of the body, and the life everlasting."

"There is only one excuse for living," writes Leon Bloy, that fiercely passionate pilgrim in search of God, "to await the Resurrection of the dead." If we speak of life as a journey, a road to be entered upon and traveled along, then we are obliged to consider three distinct phases: it begins; it ends; and in between there exists the present moment (which, even as I write the word, falls haplessly away). Eschatology, then, is simply the effort to illumine the mystery of the End, before which we are to anneal ourselves in hope. And hope, of course, remains so peculiarly and prototypically human that no one can live without it. Hope should not be confused with mere optimism, incidentally, whose reach is far less deep. Those who have hope really do look beyond the boredom, the horror, and the futility, their lives wedded to an absolutely adamantine certainty that darkness and evil need not have the last word.

I think of that marvelous ending of a story written by John Updike, "Pigeon Feathers," one of his earliest, in which a boy named David is forced to shoot some pigeons in his barn; and as he watches, transfixed, as feather upon feather floats to the ground, we see him "robed in this certainty: that the God who had lavished such craft upon these worthless birds would not destroy His whole creation by refusing to let David live forever."

I think also of that magnificent line from Franz Kafka, found on the very last page of Luigi Giussani's *The Religious Sense*. Giussani cites this line as evidence of the greatness of man: "Even if salvation does not come, still I want to be worthy of it in every instant."

Only someone alive with longing, galvanized by an obscure yet persisting hope, could say that. It is the virtue of remaining stubbornly rooted in the belief that reality is forever open to something—indeed, to someone—infinitely more. This someone is so determined on securing an indestructible joy and happiness for those he loves that to be the recipient of such love causes one to rise each morning with a lightness of sprit, a spring in the step, wonderfully reminiscent of the "tiny girl" in the famous poem by Charles Peguy, "The Portal of the Mystery of the Second Virtue," whom he enshrines as the very centerpiece of hope. "She rises every morning," he tells us, her heart radiant with the promises of God. Similarly, the little child whom G. K. Chesterton extols who sees the world in the light of an "eternal morning . . . which has a sort of wonder in it as if the world were as new as the child herself." What was so wonderful about childhood, Chesterton tells us, "is that anything in it was a wonder. It was not merely a world full of miracles; it was a miraculous world."

Hope, then, is the virtue we rightly associate with the very young, with those who look always to the beginning. "The only joy in the world," says Cesare Pavese, "is to begin. It is beautiful to live because to live is to begin, always, and every instant." And, really, how can Pavese say that unless there were, very deep down, the sense that somehow life is full of promise, flush with sheer lyric expectancy, and that in each moment life is poised to begin afresh, inviting us to unpack the secret treasures of each day as though they were gifts from another world. Right at the heart of what it means to be human, we stumble upon unmistakable evidence of an impulse that, like St. Augustine's "restless heart," is both exigent and persisting, and that always cries out for more. It is like an unseen twitch upon the thread of our lives, always plucking at our sleeve, jump-starting the spirit to move in a direction beyond this or that quotidian limit. It is as if an irrepressibility of spirit were inscribed deep down, revealing itself in ways that mere circumstance cannot intimidate, urging us to go out and fashion a more perfect future. We treat life as if it were, in that lovely phrase from the poet John Keats, "a vale of soul-making." Tomorrow thus enters decisively into today, in order to give imaginative shape to the texture of all we think, feel, or say.

Each of us is a kind of Orpheus, I like to think, who will not suffer those we love to go down into the pit unaccompanied by those who love them.

Real hope, then, is neither cheap grace nor facile optimism; instead, as the Church itself insists, it is a determination of will wholly to anchor our lives in God, on whose promised salvation we depend— like children who find all their fears banished in the sudden warmth of a word spoken, a gesture given, by the mother and father who love them. It is like the saintly Thérèse, who, as she lay dying, was asked what she would do were she suddenly to die without benefit of Viaticum, which she had so clearly longed to receive. With great serenity of heart, she answers that, if it should please God to deny her this consolation, then that too would be a grace. Because, she says simply, "Everything is grace" ("Tout est grace").

Nothing, it seems, can escape the net thrown by an all-enveloping grace given us by God in the form of hope. And in its reaching out to catch us—however seemingly, desperately lost—grace rescues us from a final fall. Yes, of course, but how exactly does one hope in something unseen, in a God no one has ever seen? But is that strictly true? Hasn't he become concretely incarnate in One who bears a distinct name? In point of fact, has he not come so scandalously close that we can reach out and kill him?

These are very deep waters. And yet, is it not passing strange how many there are who evince not the slightest interest in putting out into the deep?

CHAPTER ❹

Certain things, the loss of which would surely devastate most believers, seem not to disturb the inveterate unbeliever at all. The absence of an afterlife, for instance. The inference, of course, is that those untouched by tremors of an ultimate bliss, who have neither time nor zest for God, can never aspire as high as those who have set their sights on "the city which is to come" (Heb 13:14). Not to have faith, then, indeed deliberately to divest oneself of an inherited faith, is to have so contracted the compass of one's hope that the limit of desire extends only as far as the world one knows, the finite structures of which will sooner or later implode. What a sadness this must mean for those whose sensibilities have so flattened themselves out as to resemble nothing more than a road map stripped of any gradation whatsoever.

On the other hand, while the reach of hope will never be so lofty as to encompass an eternity with God, the corresponding temptation to despair needn't include keeping company with the devil, either. Looking into the abyss, in other words, is never too perilous for those without faith. In fact, the temptation rather is to turn the whole thing into a theme park: neither an ascent too high, nor a descent too low. It sounds like a recipe for flat bread. ("Give us this day our daily flat bread!"—would that be the perfect prayer for people who prefer everything flat? Yes, but to whom do they address the petition?) Instead of the poetry of the transcendent, one opts for the prose of the trite. Rather than hear the melodies of God and be thus lifted into realms of celestial bliss, one descends into the cacophonies of the city of *Dis*— forget the beatific; just pass me a soporific. As Josef Pieper remarks in his masterful study *On Hope*: "It makes a great difference, then, whether it is a Christian or a heathen who says: It will turn out badly for mankind, for us, for me myself."

Nihilism, in other words, has gone mainstream. "Having come to take nullity for granted," observed

Lionel Trilling, dissecting the mindset of his increasingly postmodern students, they want "to be enlightened and entertained by statements about the nature of nothing, what its size is, how it is furnished, what services the management provides, what sort of conversation and amusements can go on in it." Welcome to *Seinfeld*, where shows about nothing are a specialty of the house. In other words, let us by all means look into the abyss but only if it can be shown to be amusing. Or as the deconstructionists might say, how wonderful it is to do away with truth, because then one is spared the hard work of trying to be right, leaving only the necessity of trying to be funny. The late Richard Rorty, for example, despite having enjoyed a lucrative career teaching philosophy, was a man madly bent on destroying the discipline of philosophy itself, which he set about doing precisely by doing away with reality. And how did he define reality? In short, he defined it as so many constructs arbitrarily imposed by philosophers. "You can still find philosophy professors," he admits with incredulity, "who will solemnly tell you that they are seeking *the truth*," but it's no easy job digging up the bones of such dinosaurs. Happily, of course, the task of trying to locate "a real live metaphysical prig" (someone, that is, who actually believes in the real and thinks it important to learn the truth of it) will soon become a thing of the past now that we live in a world where, as the former Cardinal Ratzinger put it on the eve of the conclave that would elect him pope, the tyranny of relativism reigns supreme.

How far we've come from the poets and pilgrims who rail against the dying of the light. These are antique people of such antediluvian "philosophical machismo," to quote Rorty's snooty put-down of old-fashioned truth seekers, that they actually think it not only permissible to try and hitch their wagons to a star but also absolutely imperative that one spend one's life in ardent pursuit of the whole Milky Way. "Where is God? Where is God now?" It is the question Whittaker Chambers, for instance, once put to his friend William F. Buckley Jr. in a letter in which he vowed, "I shall go on dogging this point past bearing. For, indeed, it is the only crucial point of our time, and all else, wars, peace, social and political systems, dwindle beside it."

Here one thinks especially of the figure of poor, God-obsessed Gerard Manley Hopkins, S.J., author of the "terrible sonnets," who, having sunk to the lowest point of his soul's distress, registers such heartrending absence of God ("I wake and feel the fell of dark, not day") that the reader's own heart nearly breaks on this seeming wheel of divine indifference.

> With witness I speak this. But where
>   I say
> Hours I mean years, mean life. And
>   my lament
> Is cries countless, cries like dead
>   letters sent
> To dearest him that lives alas! away.

"A terrible pathos" his friend George Dixon found in them, suggesting the poet's own experience of the fear of being separated from God forever. "I am gall, I am heartburn," the second stanza begins. "God's most deep decree / Bitter would have me taste: my taste was me." And yet, to be sure, the sense here of permanent spiritual loss, an intimation even of that final hopelessness that is first cousin to despair ("I see," the sonnet ends, "The lost are like this, and their scourge to be / As I am mine, their sweating selves; but worse"), can also be, as the great mystics assure us, an essential moment in the soul's ascent to God. And, yes, Hopkins himself appeared to have made that ascent at the very last, following upon the impacted dryness and desolation of which the sonnets speak, as witness words he spoke on his deathbed in the last moments of his life: "I am so happy, so happy."

Nevertheless, we mustn't, as Plato himself warns, move too quickly from the many to the one or, to paraphrase a line from *The Suffering of Love* (that is, the book the dissertation became), go too glibly from Good Friday to Easter Sunday. How tempting it is to move that march at breakneck speed; yet to do so is to miss all the dark and necessary music in between, namely, the Mystery of Holy Saturday itself. So, however dolorous the melodic line, let us press the question to yet another crisis point, asking if there might not be a final and still greater horror awaiting us on the other side. What if God himself were not to be found there? Suppose all those letters so plaintively sent by the poet Hopkins all come back unread because there is no God to read them?

When Alfred Delp, the German Jesuit priest martyred by the Nazis, was about to be hanged, his last words, whispered jokingly to the prison chaplain who accompanied him to the gallows, were as follows: "In half-an-hour, I'll know more than you." Yes, but perhaps not. What if he was wrong; what then? If there is neither God nor heaven, who then will have the last laugh?

We are reminded by Hans Urs von Balthasar that God is so intensely alive that he can afford to be dead. But, again, suppose none of this were true. Suppose it were only possible for us human beings to imagine, as John Lennon famously invited us to do, a world without heaven, without God, the skies shorn of every trace of the sacred, the existence of God only a whispered, unfounded rumor? "It's easy if you try," he assures us. "No hell below us / Above us only sky / Imagine all the people living for today."

It would be a perfect hell to imagine such a place, never mind Lennon having vaporized all traces thereof, and still more so if one were forced to inhabit it. Is there anyone out there—this side of Dr. Kevorkian, that is—who's actually looking forward to extinction? Can there be any percentage in nothingness? "Despite every possibility of falling into nothingness," declares Professor Pieper in his book *On Hope*, "the proper orientation of the 'way' is toward being—to such an extent that, to be possible, even the decision in favor of nothingness would have to wear the mask of a decision for being." So much for the parasitic nature of nothingness, feeding on the very thing it rejects. The point is the prospect of only an empty sky above us, followed by an eternity of black annihilation, hasn't really got a whole lot to commend, at least not to those of us who long for the company of others. And, of course, it is only on the fixed assumption of God's existence, on the truth, goodness, and beauty of his being God, that any of us will find on the other side those whom we have loved and lost on this one.

Ah, but isn't this precisely the rub? While I may hope with all my heart to join hands with those dearest departed—to look once again and forever upon the face of my mother, my brother, and my father—in the end it is only hope, the thinnest of reeds, that sustains my longing for them, not the certainty of knowledge—at least not the same order of knowledge that guarantees, for instance, the sum of two plus two will always equal four. Now there is a datum on which even the most hardened skeptics would stake their lives. But hope? Why, it's only "the thing with feathers," as Emily Dickinson would say, "That perches in the soul, / And sings the tune without the words, / And never stops at all." How gossamer a thing is that? To what impossible chimera of desire has it not given illusory flight? A thing with feathers is no better than Shakespeare's "walking shadow, a poor player / That struts and frets his hour upon the stage / And then is heard no more." Indeed, a thing with feathers, one is constrained sorrowfully to admit, is no better, no more dependable, than the wax wings on which poor Icarus launched himself into space.

Let's face it. We've entered the world of the subjunctive, an almost unreal place where we're likely to find that "subtle glutton," whom Miss Dickinson designates as hope, feeding upon the fair and unsuspecting who presumably haven't the kidney to face the night. "And yet," she warns, "inspected closely, / What abstinence is there!" Hope is not very giving, in other words. And so we mustn't forget that here in the realm of the subjunctive everything is but a mood, not a tense indicating when or what will happen. It carries no real freight, only the hope and the desire that, please God, things might turn out well in the end. A writer by the name of Michele Morano, in a fine essay called "Grammar Lessons," has called it "the mood of mystery. Of luck. Of faith interwoven with doubt. It's a held breath, a hand reaching out, carefully touching wood. It's humility, deference, the opposite of hubris. And it's going to take a long time to master." It will have to, of course, if, as the experience of the saints and martyrs teach us, the cry of hope is always uttered by someone on whom the happy outcome of his or her hope does not finally depend.

CHAPTER ❺

In a splendid collection of poems entitled *Anterooms* by two-time Pulitzer Prize winner Richard Wilbur—who is nearly ninety, by the way, and still banging out some of the finest blooms in the business—the theme of longing emerges early on and, like a wide ribbon, wraps itself brightly round the whole volume. My favorite is a lovely little thing called "The House," in which a grieving widower remembers a dream his dead wife would often have of a white house seen luminously in the distance, yet always just out of reach. He is powerfully drawn to this image—it has come to haunt his own dreams—seeing it as emblematic of the promise and possibility of a place where death can no longer touch those we love. "Is she now there," he asks, "wherever there may be?"

> Only a foolish man would hope to
>   find
> That haven fashioned by her
>   dreaming mind.
> Night after night, my love, I put to
>   sea.

How easy it is to give such sentiments a cheap, cyni-
cal spin, trivializing the search for an unreal house
where, even now, a dead wife awaits a husband at
sea looking to find her. Doesn't he realize that it is
all quite hopeless, a quest both futile and imbecilic?
Why should he, to quote Shakespeare, "trouble deaf
Heaven with [his] bootless cries"? Is it because he
does not really believe heaven to be deaf to such cries?
From where could that notion have come? And, if
he thought the effort to make contact completely
pointless and silly, why does he address the poem to
someone who, despite knowing her to be dead, he
yet speaks to as though she were still living? "Night
after night," he tells her, the wife he cannot let go
of, whom he will not consign to the forgetfulness of
death, "I put to sea."

C. S. Lewis, in a profound passage on hope from
his classic work *Mere Christianity*, reminds us that
if creatures are born with certain desires, it must

follow that nature will make provision for their satisfaction. "A baby feels hunger: well, there is such a thing as food." Ducks, he tells us, have the desire to swim, so there must be water, right? Ah, but if nature proves unequal to a given desire, what then? Are we expected to simply suppress the desire? Here Lewis is wonderfully encouraging. "If I find in myself a desire which no experience in this world can satisfy, the most probable explanation is that I was made for another world." And if one were to suppress *that* desire, which is the deepest of all desires that drive the human heart—to wit, desire for an everlasting joy no less—refusing to believe that anyone could reach the rainbow's end, what a disaster it would be "to find out too late (a moment after death) that by our supposed 'common sense' we had stifled in ourselves the faculty of enjoying it."

So that's it? Yes, but how exactly does one go about proving it? It is hardly enough, is it, in the case of the grieving husband putting out to sea, to establish the existence of the fabled house merely because he desires it to be? To go from the optative to the declarative mood is just that, a mood; it is not a demonstration of anything, certainly not a datum on which apodictic certainty can be found. Maybe what

the husband really needs is a good therapist, someone
to shepherd him through the grieving process, teach
him some coping strategies, and suggest another wife
perhaps, someone nubile enough to outlive *him*.

What he really needs is someone to tell him the
truth, which is that the longing and desire for the
wife he has lost, far from being idle and ineffectual,
is in point of fact perfectly natural, even as nothing
in nature exists to fulfill it. It cannot be placated by
an appeal to mere memory, since it is clearly not in
the realm of memory that he's looking for her. It is
the extramental reality of the wife he's lost that he so
longs to have restored. And, finally, most extraordinary of all, the search for this missing wife is not subject to an ultimate frustration. Indeed, as the teaching
of St. Thomas Aquinas reveals, its very fulfillment is
entirely realizable on the basis of hope. The question
is as follows: what precisely are the blessings we ought
to hope to obtain from God? The Common Doctor
gives this answer:

> One, before a thing can be hoped for,
> it must first be desired. Things that are
> not desired are not said to be objects
> of hope; rather they are feared or even
> despised. Two, we must judge that what

is hoped for is possible to obtain; hope includes this factor over and above desire. True, a man can desire things he does not believe he is able to attain; but he cannot cherish hope with regard to such objects. Three, hope necessarily implies the idea that the good hoped for is hard to get: trifles are the object of contempt rather than of hope.

So where do matters stand now? So utterly real is this deep, persisting—surprisingly fierce even—exigency of the soul, this stirring and surge of the heart on first awakening to the possibilities of hope, that it really does succeed—yes, even in the face of its own seeming impossibility—in effecting the very object of our hope.

The hydraulics of hope, you might say, are eternal. The sheer irrepressibility of the one who hopes, like a hidden stream deep within the heart, is able to course its way right straight into the abyss of death, there to retrieve those who are lost, restoring them all to the arms of God. Nowhere, of course, is this more undeniably the case than when it comes to those we love. And here we touch the heart of the matter, what the philosopher Gabriel Marcel in *The Philosophy of Existentialism* has called "the ontological mystery."

> To hope against all hope that a person whom I love will recover [say] from a disease which is said to be incurable is to say: It is impossible that I should be alone in willing this cure; it is impossible that reality in its inward depth should be hostile or so much as indifferent to what I assert is in itself a good.

Here is an exercise in the audacity of hope no bolder than which can be imagined. It is entirely beside the point, I take Marcel to be saying, were one to adduce whole busloads of evidence to the contrary, citing this or that redundant case study where, alas, the patients all died. In the teeth of the assertion itself, all objections fall haplessly away. "I assert . . . that reality is on my side in willing it to be so," insists Marcel. "I do not wish: I assert; such is the prophetic tone of true hope."

One cannot help but think here of all those biblical scenes, where astonishment and fear lay hold of the crowd, as Jesus, the air electric with expectation, stoops to raise the dead to life. "Do not weep," he tells the grieving mother whose dead son is effortlessly restored to her. Or we think of the disconsolate Martha, sister to poor Lazarus who dies, going at once to remonstrate with Jesus who, had he only been there sooner, could have saved him. And Jesus, who is himself moved to tears by the death of his friend, straightaway enjoins the dead man to get up.

Thou shalt not die! Isn't that what love, real love of the other, most deeply and insistently demands? "All joy wills eternity," exclaims Friedrich Nietzsche, "wills deep, deep eternity." What an amazing admission from so godless a source! The atheist philosopher confesses with abject terror: "God is dead! God will stay dead! And we have killed him!" No wonder the poor man went mad.

But, again, on what possible basis besides hope—which is the very voice of prayer, of desire transmuted in the fire of love before being lifted up to God—do we profess to know anything at all about these matters? Well, what is prayer? It is someone who has nothing asking God for everything. The poet Emily Dickinson describes it as "the little implement / Through which men reach / Where presence is denied them. / They fling their speech / By means of it in God's ear." And like the poor beggar whose arms remain outstretched, they humbly await God to fill their emptiness.

In Blessed John Paul II's *The Jeweler's Shop*, a play of luminous, unforgettable beauty, a young Polish priest consoles the widow of his dearest friend, who bravely gave his life resisting the Nazi takeover of their country, telling her that her husband is *more alive now* than ever he might have been in the flesh. She accepts this, not because she knows it to be true, but rather because she believes, she hopes—*desperately desires*—that it may be so. What else are we but sheer hunger and thirst for all that we cannot have, this finite being armed with infinite desires. So there we stand, arms stretched high into the sky, against the howling wind, crying out, awaiting the One who alone can come to rescue and restore all whom he has loved and lost. We simply cannot know to what unimaginable lengths, day by day, we go, inching our way into the kingdom.

From a wistful fragment entered into a slim volume compiled by the critic Alfred Kazin—its title, *A Lifetime Burning in Every Moment*, is taken from T. S. Eliot's *Four Quartets*—he confesses to being "refreshed by writers ancient and modern who speak confidently of their belief in God," notwithstanding the great difficulty he has of doing so in a world where "the distance from God to man is so wide that I have never had a revelation." And yet, he says, ending on a note of unvanquished hope, there are wonderful discoveries to be made, among them the following from Karl Rahner, whom he invokes with gratitude:

> If human beings are hungry for meaning, that is a result of the existence of God. If God does not exist, the hunger is absurd. The hunger is a longing that cannot be satisfied. A longing for God cannot be taken away. Man is a being who does not live absurdly—because he loves, he hopes, and because God, the holy mystery, is infinitely receptive and accepting of him.

The key, once more, is prayer. And, again, what is prayer but the courtesy God confers when inviting us to the dignity of becoming a cause of that for which we pray. Nothing less will pry loose the planks that seal us off from the world where the dead dwell, those we long for communion with, the blessed ones whom we await in hope on the other side. As St. Thomas Aquinas teaches, "what we cannot do by ourselves, we can do through our friends," chief of whom is Jesus Christ, who first blazed the trail to the place of the dead in order to free all the souls held hostage in the kingdom of night. Prayer, then, is the hard currency we spend, not only to negotiate our own way home, but also to build bridges to those who have already crossed over, joining rank upon rank of the grateful dead in that great web of glory that awaits us all. "We die with the dying," says Eliot.

> See, they depart, and we go with
>   them.
> We are born with the dead:
> See, they return, and bring us with
>   them.
> The moment of the rose and the
>   moment of the yew-tree
> Are of equal duration.

CHAPTER ❻

Here is a story, endlessly instructive, as told by the late Monsignor Luigi Giussani, founder of Communion and Liberation, a movement that has mushroomed in recent years, particularly among young people for whom the hunger and thirst for God, for ultimate truth, beauty, and happiness, cries out for a fulfillment that nothing in this world can match. Only Christ can answer the longings of the human heart in a way that finally satisfies. It is a story he has recounted in several places, including at the very end of his book *The Religious Sense*. It provides an ideal point of entry for a reflection on what I have been calling *desperate desire*.

The story itself, he tells us, touches on an experience he had many years before, an experience whose impact would prove so immense and far-reaching that it became the defining theme of his life, his work. It amounted to a sort of signature statement, a benchmark to identify, to summarize, the meaning of his being.

"Once, as a very young man," he begins, "I got lost in the great wood of Tradate . . . and, in the grip of panic, I shouted for a full three hours as the sun sank in the sky. That experience made me see—afterwards—that man is search; man is search if he cries out. . . ."

Now I haven't a clue as to what or where this forest of Tradate is (perhaps it is in the north of Italy, near Milan, the region where he was born and spent most of his life); and I suspect it must be a deep, dark, and dense forest, a wholly sinister setting in which to be lost. And, to be sure, only an Italian is capable of producing three hours of full-throated shouting.

But where is Giussani going with this? What is he getting at? He is saying only this: to be human, to aspire to the meaning of what fundamentally defines our humanity, is to be someone whose whole life can only be understood in terms of *search*. That fundamental fact, it would appear, is axiomatic, the linchpin on which all life turns. Without it, that pesky little pin, the wheel falls off. So life is to be understood as search, as quest, an exploration in constant search of the truth about ourselves and about the world in which we find ourselves. "What is the formula," asks Giussani, "for the journey to the ultimate meaning of reality?" The answer is "living the real."

In order for us to be wholly alive, therefore, fully engaged in the business of being, we must have this eagerness to explore, to seek out all the lineaments of the mystery, sounding their depths as though our very lives depended upon it. Life as sheer hunger and thirst. Man, says Plato, is a child of poverty. The plate is always empty.

All of this sharpens the sense that there really is a reason—indeed, it qualifies as supremely, personally compelling—to justify the search. One does not ordinarily embark upon an empty quest. And what exactly is the reason? It is the fact that you are quite simply lost. And the sudden realization of that fact, of the bloody fix you're in, puts you at once in the throes of a panic. So you cry out. What else can you do? And, by the way, you are in very good company.

Your situation is exactly parallel to that of the great Dante, premier pilgrim-poet of the Christian West, who, finding himself alone in a dark wood in the middle of the journey of *his* life, was likewise moved to cry out. So put yourself imaginatively alongside poor Dante, the result of whose predicament, incidentally, has become one of those rare and imperishable monuments of world literature.

It is the afternoon of Good Friday in the year 1300 and Dante Alighieri is thirty-five years of age. "Midway in our life's journey," he tells us on the very first page of the *Divine Comedy*,

> I went astray from the straight road
>   and woke to find myself
> alone in a dark wood. How shall I say
> what wood that was! I never saw so
>   drear,
> so rank, so arduous a wilderness!
> Its very memory gives a shape to
>   fear.
> Death could scarce be more bitter
>   than that place!

Think of it . . . a place so dismal, so deeply, unrelievedly bleak—indeed, of such profound and acute dread—that even death itself could not have been more bitter! So what does one do in a situation of lostness but cry out? One has simply got to cry out, to externalize the fear. How else do we find out where we are if we don't scream? We certainly can't keep it to ourselves. In short, each of us is a kind of castaway who, perhaps by some strange mischance of fate, a bout of bad karma, as it were, has fallen from the sky. I think of that silly Tom Hanks movie of some years back, showing some poor guy literally falling out of an airplane onto a beach where, among other absurdities, he develops a relationship with a volleyball.

Not recommended.

Or put it this way: we are beggars ("the true protagonist of history," Giussani tells us, "is the beggar") who must cry out for all that we do not have. It is not that our glass is half full, and perhaps a kind waiter might freshen our drink. No, the glass is entirely empty. And so, amid "the parched, eviscerate soil," of which the poet T. S. Eliot speaks, our roots need rain. Thus it is not really possible to stifle the cry. If it is not to leave us gasping for breath, strangled in our very soul, we must declaim our hunger and thirst. We trumpet it to the heavens—yes, even if, as experience all too redundantly shows, our cries be "bootless" and, alas, no one seems to come.

In a scene from Ingmar Bergman's *The Seventh Seal*, a haunting tale set in a medieval world, we see the character of the knight go down on his knees before an open confessional, addressing the hooded figure behind the grill (it is Death), telling him how hard it is to find God. "I want knowledge, not faith, not suppositions, but knowledge. I want God to stretch out his hand toward me, reveal himself and speak to me." But Death does not speak. The cry of the knight, meanwhile, continues: "I call out to him in the dark, but no one seems to be there." To which Death at last replies, dagger drawn as if to strike at the heart: "Perhaps no one is there." To this intended fatal thrust, the knight responds as only a person can whose desire has grown dangerously desperate: "Then life is an outrageous horror. No one can live in the face of death, knowing that all is nothingness."

Ah, but here, I do most devoutly believe, Giussani would disagree. Because, he would argue, there is yet another and still deeper consideration at work: the experience of being lost, seemingly, hopelessly, and forever—says Giussani, besides revealing us as pure search, as one the whole thrust of whose being lost simply must cry out—testifies at the same time to a real if mysterious certainty of *another*. There is, you see, in every circumstance of loss, of being lost, a genuine intimation, however impalpable, of the presence of *someone* who can actually hear the cry of one who is lost. "The cry," he insists, "implies the existence of something other." Otherwise, why would people cry out at all?

Is that clear? If nobody is there, why on earth would you cry out? It is quite horrible enough just being frightened out of one's skin. But who wants to look ridiculous as well? "The very existence of the question," says Giussani, "implies the existence of an answer." And why is that? This is so because

> expectation is the very structure of our nature, it is the essence of our soul. It is not something calculated: it is given. For the *promise* is at the origin, from the very origin of our creation. He who has made man has also made him as "promise." *Structurally* man waits; structurally he is a beggar; structurally life is promise.

Isn't this finally the reason there must be a God: that this insistent, desperate desire for a way out of the forest will someday, someway, find fulfillment—and that all the questions put to what appears to be only a blank and indifferent sky will, nevertheless, be finally answered in the *you of another*? "Thus Faith," as Joseph Ratzinger movingly reminds us in *Introduction to Christianity*,

> is the finding of a "You" that bears me up and amid all the unfulfilled—and in the last resort unfulfillable—hope of human encounters gives me the promise of an indestructible love which not only longs for eternity but guarantees it. Christian faith lives on the discovery that not only is there such a thing as objective meaning, but this meaning knows me and loves me, I can entrust myself to it like the child that knows all its questions answered in the "you" of its mother.

In other words, there really is an answer to this cry; indeed, the more desperate the cry for help, the more certain we are of an answer. But the answer does not come out of any sort of thing we might devise (a compass, say), whose usefulness is seen at once to be equal to our predicament. The state of being lost is simply not amenable to solution in mechanical terms. Escape can only come from the outside, from above. Escape comes from a source transcendent to the mess, that is, One who is himself not lost (indeed, being God, he is never lost), and yet, having submitted himself to a state of being lost like us, is thus able to identify with his lost brother and so effect the rescue our hearts so insistently cry out for. We are all lost. There are no exceptions to the desolation we experience, the fearful desperation it arouses. And it is only the event of Jesus Christ, who comes into the flesh of sin in order precisely to free us from its malice and misery, that can lift us finally onto the plane of grace and glory.

There is one final point, which is the most startling of all: the very nature of the rescue offered by Christ, when it erupts into our world, bursting through the ceiling of our lives, all at once exceeds every conceivable expectation we have that—somehow, someway—we shall be saved. This means that a life sustained by hope, a life whose scaffolding rests upon the expectation that everything will turn out well in the end (again, to recall those unutterably beautiful words spoken by Jesus to Lady

Julian of Norwich, "All shall be well and all manner of thing shall be well"), suddenly and unac-
countably discovers a fulfillment totally surpassing
even the highest and loftiest possibilities of human
expectation.

> I did not know my longing, till I
>   encountered You.
> I see what freedom is; Your plan
>   prepared for me.
> I will not search for more because
> You will save me now.[7]

The castaway, you see, is *every person*. Or, at the very
least, people who possess by some inscrutable grace
the certainty of the awareness that they are castaways,
lost in the great forest of being, yet strangely aware
of a way out. The very path Christ himself first made
through that forest the rest of us are now free to
follow.

Christianity, then, is really nothing other than an
event that each of us is meant to encounter. It is
a radically new and unforeseen happening in the
great sea of history. And, to be sure, what is most
symptomatic about it, the feature that fairly leaps
off the page, is the discovery we make that precisely
in Christ, in the human form assumed by God, we

see and experience the pure mercy of Our Father in heaven.

Here is a lovely passage from St. Augustine that sums up, incomparably, all that I have been trying to say:

> You were walking in your own way, a vagabond straying through wooded places, through rugged places, torn in all your limbs. You were seeking a home and you did not find it. There came to you the way itself and you were set therein. Walk by Him, the Man, and you come to God.[8]

CHAPTER ❼

Leaving aside the few friends whose names and faces even now, nearly a half century later, time cannot entirely erase, I remember almost nothing of my high school years. As some wag once wrote of the sixties, if you can remember them, you must not have been there. And so neither the classes I attended, nor the poor devils who taught them, have left much of an impression.

If it wasn't for the diploma collecting dust in some forgotten storage bin, no doubt covering over the Davy Crockett cap I could never bring myself to pitch, or that unflattering senior photo in the year-book I never bought, it might be difficult to prove I'd ever gone to high school at all. But one image from that distant time remains seared upon my memory.

It was 1962, the year Marilyn Monroe and Eleanor Roosevelt died, and there I was, a callow sixteen-year-old, sitting in an auditorium at a school assembly listening to an old rabbi recount the lives of those two celebrated women, each so utterly unlike the other that it seemed almost impossible to imagine they had occupied the same planet. Yet he managed to draw them together so poignantly that to this day I cannot separate them in my mind.

It was not their lives, however, which could hardly have been more disparate, but the fact of death itself that formed the link between them. The precise image the rabbi used to describe this connection was that of two freshly interred corpses undergoing an identical decomposition of flesh. Imagine Edgar Alan Poe's "Conquering Worm" wrapping itself about the bodies of each, emitting the ooze of a final, consuming corruption. Or the *Danse Macabre* of late medieval art, in which figures both rich and poor, radiant and wretched, are equally conscripted to move remorselessly toward death. The imagery could scarcely appear more repulsive—or riveting. Neither the glitter of the Hollywood star, nor the gawkiness of the Hyde Park humanitarian, would make the slightest bit of difference the moment they were lowered into the ground. The uniform hideousness of death would grind their flesh equally fine.

Was it this episode that catalyzed my own accumulating interest in the subject of death, a curiosity so lively that it has spilled over into books and essays and countless course syllabi? Or perhaps it was a certain portrait of a doomed relative, her loveliness caught with an almost luminous perfection in an old photograph that hung above the stairwell of my childhood home, taken not long before she died of consumption. She was the aunt my mother never knew, and on her youthful face I would sometimes look for signs of death. I was always seeing the skull beneath the skin, to pilfer a fine phrase from the poetry of T. S. Eliot, which he ascribes to John Webster, an Elizabethan dramatist, an able contemporary of Shakespeare. "Webster was much possessed by death / And saw the skull beneath the skin; / And breastless creatures under ground / Leaned backward with a lipless grin."

But then, why be a Christian if not to escape such evils? Who wants to die? I mean, really, what percentage can there be in the embrace of death? "Oh, sure,

just put me in that little box; then tuck me into the
cozy ground where worms and maggots feed on my
flesh! Are you crazy?" And it will surely do no good
to take refuge in the fact that the dead, being dead,
will never know what it's like to be dead. Because
it is the idea of death, and the image with which
we clothe the thought, that produces the torment,
the sudden sense of shuddering horror that will not
go away. Take poor Claudio, for instance, in Shakespeare's *Measure for Measure*, for whom the prospect
of having to die proves so unnerving that he is willing
even to betray his own sister in order to escape it:

> Ay, but to die, and go we know
>   not where,
> To lie in cold obstruction and
>   to rot,
> This sensible warm motion
>   to become
> A kneaded clod; and the delighted
>   spirit
> To bathe in fiery floods, or to reside
> In thrilling region of thick-ribbed
>   ice;
> To be imprisoned in the viewless
>   winds,

And blown with restless violence
   round about
The pendant world; or to be worse
   than worst
Of those that lawless and incertain
   thought
Imagine howling:—'tis too
   horrible!
The weariest and most loathed
   worldly life
That age, ache, penury, and
   imprisonment
Can lay on nature is a paradise
To what we fear of death.[9]

Despite all the pleasures of the intervening play, there is not a sentient being alive who does not instinctively recoil from the last act, knowing it will invariably prove bloody. In short, none of us is exempt from that final nightfall, through the silence of which we shall all someday pass. Entirely alone, we shall pass through the door and into the house of death, which admits only one at a time; we've all been scheduled to go through it. "Someday," writes Karl Barth, "a company of men will process out to a churchyard and lower a coffin and everyone will go home; but one will not come back, and that will be me. The seal of death will be that they will bury me as a thing that is superfluous and disturbing in the land of the living."

Make no mistake about it—death is the supreme evil. As John Webster himself writes, "On pain of death, let no man name death to me: It is a word infinitely terrible." Taken from *The White Devil*, the line is spoken by a character named Brachiano, who is himself destined to suffer a most horrible death. On this side of the grave, then, death is rightly seen as *the* enemy. This leaves only the ultimate horror, to wit, an eternity shorn of the company of God, namely, hell itself, no greater evil imaginable.

But death, for all its grisliness and sting, cannot be given, at least not for the Christian, the last word. After all, as the hymn says, we are Easter people and Alleluia is our song. How, I wonder, are we to reconcile these tensions, to sustain hope in the teeth of all that we know of death? The most doleful fact is that the Old Guy will not be kept waiting indefinitely, nor will his summons prove especially pleasant to those who think it possible to put him off. "Like as the waves make towards the pebbled shore," says Shakespeare, "So do our minutes hasten to their end." With each rise and fall of the sea—the dread, implacable sea—we are drawn nearer and nearer to death.

And so there surely is a sense in which these matters cannot be reconciled. Rather, like any mystery, they must be endured. Death, the final cancellation toward which I am moving even as I type these words, was never a problem any of us could solve. There are no extant blueprints on how to build a bypass around the city of death; it remains the necessary terminus for every traveler. The tension will simply not go away. Like the Cross of Christ, it remains as paradox. I think of that splendid poem by Gerard Manley Hopkins, "That Nature Is a Heraclitean Fire and of the Comfort of the Resurrection"—its very title neatly emblematic of the tension that refuses facile resolution. The destruction of all life, of which the fire promised by Heraclitus serves as an apt symbol, must be given its due. Even death has a kind of integrity. And in the unvarying collision it has with life, death appears always to win. "Man, how fast his firedint, his mark on mind, is gone! / Both are in an unfathomable, all is in an enormous dark / Drowned. O pity and indignation!"

We are right to feel indignant, yes—but wrong to think our indignation might allow us to escape the encircling doom. Heraclitus knew this, of course; he lived in a world oppressed by the sadness of life, of a life without the joy Christ conferred simply by his coming among us. And so, says Hopkins, giving that great and tragic pre-Socratic pessimist his due, "Flesh fade, and mortal trash / Fall to the residuary worm; world's wildfire, leave but ash."

But to leave out what follows—the new reality wrought by the redemption of Jesus Christ . . . "Christus totam novitatem attulit, semetipsum afferens," exclaims the sainted bishop and martyr Irenaeus ("Christ brought all things new by bringing himself.")—would be an injustice to the God who vanquished death by his Son's willingness to endure it. "See," says the resurrected Jesus, "I make all things new!" Indeed, he goes all the way to hell in his determination to atone for sin, to make all things new. This is why the Church deliberately inserted the event of Christ's Descent at the very center of the creed. The sheer intensity of Jesus's life is such that he can undergo real death, descending into the silence and the shame of Sheol in order to bring back the prisoners of death, with whom the triumph of Easter Sunday then takes place. And so the last lines of the poem belong not to the Heraclitean but to the Pentecostal fire of the Holy Ghost. "In a flash, at a trumpet crash," exclaims Hopkins, "I am all at once what Christ is, since he was what I am, and / This Jack, joke, poor potsherd, patch, matchwood, immortal diamond, / Is immortal diamond."

This is the faith on which the engine of hope turns. Like a dynamo fired with sheer desperate desire, it launches out in search of that which will enable it to surmount the final desolation of death. Yet, in refusing to give Heraclitus the last word, are we maybe contriving a means of escape where none exists? In other words, how can we really be sure that God will more than make do the damages wrought by death? That even now death is being swallowed up in the greater victory wrought by Christ? "One short sleep past," declares the poet John Donne, "we wake eternally; / And death shall be no more; death thou shalt die."

Because death belongs to the order of a history bloodied by sin, a fallen order that Christ himself suffered to enter and redeem, we to whom a new order of grace has been given may thus anneal ourselves in hope. This is provided, of course, we remain grounded in a faith that, while we cannot prove the truth of it in any precise mathematical way, nevertheless we see that it perfectly corresponds to all that we most desire in the way of joy, happiness, and peace. Thus, by believing in Christ, who dared to assume our death, we affirm that he succeeded as well in delivering us from the horror and the absurdity of it. And, no, this is not anything we know; rather, it is something we believe. Or rather, someone whom we believe: the human being Jesus, in whom the whole meaning of being has all at once become flesh. It is on the sheer rock of that mystery of faith that you and I are able freely to move in Christian hope.

CHAPTER ⓼

How very nice, I can hear the chorus of cynics, chirping away in the distance. But, surely, it is nothing more than wishful thinking. How can a mere mood, however indomitable the desire on which it draws, possibly portend, in moments fraught with great sadness and loss, a final victory over death and despair? When the writer Albert Camus assures us that, "in the midst of winter, I finally learned that there was in me an invincible summer," one would like to ask him how he knows this. On what basis can he get away with saying that? Is he not stealing a base? Or maybe he intends by the statement nothing more than a figure of speech, a mere seasonal metaphor, as it were, indicating a long hoped for climate change—certainly not a reflection on the landscape of his soul.

Maybe he really isn't making large-sounding meta-physical claims at all. But if not, why then does he choose the word "invincible"? By what sleight of hand does he imagine that winter, a bleak emblem of death and dissolution, will be overcome, vanquished even, by a mere fluctuation of weather? Over what strange alchemy does Camus preside to think death in life will give way to life in death?

And while we're at it, what on earth are we to make of "Good Night, Willie Lee, I'll See You in the Morning," a poem by Alice Walker about a wife who, gazing upon the face of her dead husband for the last time, tells him without a trace of irony that, of course, she'll see him in the morning? The thing ends on a note of stunning triumph, too, imparting to the reader a "forgiveness / that permits a promise / of our return / at the end."

How can she get away with saying that? Will the dead be persuaded to come back because we've forgiven them? Surely not.

Or what about the Anglican bishop Henry King, exhorting his wife—"his matchless, never-to-be-forgotten friend"—whose death he memorializes in "The Exequy"?

Sleep on my Love in thy cold bed
Never to be disquieted! . . .
Stay for me there; I will not fail
To meet thee in that hollow vale.
And think not much of my delay;
I am already on the way.[10]

Does he really think it likely that she'll be there? That she hears him even? Indeed, he tells her, "My pulse, like a soft drum / Beats my approach, tells thee I come; / And slow howe'er my marches be, / I shall at last sit down by thee."

And, finally, there is the example of Edna St. Vincent Millay, a poet of such intense lyric and melancholy beauty that, for sheer heartbreaking pathos, she is almost without peer. A typical specimen, "Dirge Without Music," begins, "I am not resigned to the shutting away of loving hearts in the hard ground." Then, watching them each disappear into the dark— "the wise and the lovely. Crowned / With lilies and with laurel they go," never to be seen again—she repeats the sad refrain: "but I am not resigned." And while the ending, too, is full of grief and sadness, there is at the same time just the slightest hint of an intimation that, because these things are not to be borne, perhaps something really ought to be done about them. Exactly what, of course, we are never told. Still, the reader is invited, ever so slightly, to infer that these things, in some ontologically final way, shall not be given the last word. But then by whose decree will the last word be given? In other words, who ultimately is in charge of the cosmos?

> Down, down, down into the
>   darkness of the grave
> Gently they go, the beautiful, the
>   tender, the kind;
> Quietly they go, the intelligent, the
>   witty, the brave.
> I know. But I do not approve. And
>   I am not resigned.[11]

One hears in these lines, especially in the very last line with its refusal, however understated, to give in—the quiet gesture of protest it makes against the overweening power of death, of an encircling darkness that always seems to win—the voice of a resistance that could only be called supernatural, harnessed as it necessarily must be to a vision of expectation and hope finally not of this world. Otherwise, of course, we're back in paganism, in the world before Christ came to redeem it: the Greek and Roman world where, subject to the caprice and corruption of the gods, life becomes a thing unrelievedly poor and bleak. It is, moreover, the same sense of mounting doom and horror that fills so much of Elizabethan theater with an atmospheric despair virtually impossible to escape. Think only of the anguished cry of poor Gloucester, his innocent eyes freshly plucked from their sockets: "As flies to wanton boys are we to the gods; / they torture us for their sport." Here, of course, in Shakespeare's *King Lear*, is a rich and imaginative reworking of the earlier tragic ethos of the Greeks, whose dramatic formula has scarcely been improved upon since Shakespeare pronounced it "a tale told by an idiot." As the critic George Steiner remarks in *The Death of Tragedy*, "Things are as they are, unrelenting and absurd. We are punished far in excess of our guilt."

But we are not resigned to this condition, are we? For if, on the one side, we hear the voice of high pagan resignation that comes to us from Homer and Virgil, and Lucretius and Seneca—indeed, the immemorial accent of so many bent and gnarled figures of Castilian peasantry forever telling us, "No hay remedio"—we need not heed the counsel of despair that lies hidden beneath the words. For, on the other side, there remains a voice yet greater, whose message is anchored to a hope that has overcome the world. On the strength of that voice, moreover, one can make a very strong case not only for God—the fact of his existence, for instance—but for the sheer goodness of the world he made as well, by drawing precisely upon those deep reserves of hope that turn the engine of the soul.

God, we must remember, is not a problem we solve from the outside; rather, he is a mystery we are forced to endure from within. It is a question that leaves no person untouched. And, of course, the future of hope turns on the outcome of the question we put to ourselves concerning the mystery that is God. Here I think of that superb and gifted Jesuit who lived a half century or more ago, Father John Courtney Murray, who, in a series of lectures delivered at Yale in the early 1960s (later published in an elegant little book, still in print, called *The Problem of God*), has unpacked the question in a brilliant and systematic way.

How then does Father Murray proceed? Well, taking a text from Dostoyevsky, that if God were not to exist, everything would be permitted, he amends it as follows: "If God is not, no one is permitted to say or even to think that he is, for this would be a monstrous deception . . . a pernicious illusion whose result would necessarily be the destruction of man. On the other hand," he counters, "if God is, again one thing is not permitted. It is not permitted that any man should be ignorant of him, for this ignorance, too, would be the destruction of man. On both counts, therefore, no man may say that the problem of God is not his problem."

So what is the case for God, indeed for the worthwhileness of the world he made, but that, in the very mode of hope, the mood of the subjunctive, we need God in order that all the longings of the human heart may reach their supreme, optimal fulfillment? "The human being," declares Monsignor Luigi Giussani, "is properly that level of nature in which nature asks itself: 'Why do I exist?' Man is that miniscule particle which demands a meaning, a reason—the reason." Who am I, then, but a being beset by questions I may not ignore, yet cannot answer. And if there were an answer to the question that is my life—an existence briefly, heartbreakingly spent between womb and tomb—only God would be in a position to tell me. Only God can save us now, to sound the theme that so haunted the philosopher Martin Heidegger. Certainly science, for all its pretensions to exact measurable knowledge, has not cornered the market on meaning. And technological humans, of course, for all their vaunted progress in subduing those forces determined on their destruction, have yet to succeed in disarming the last enemy, which is death. And because, therefore, I am more than the sum of my parts, more than mere matter in motion, it follows that the refusal to turn to God because some clever sophist has persuaded me of his nonexistence amounts to an assault upon the most elemental dimension of my being, namely, the thirst for a total answer to the human predicament. My need for a truth finally transcendent to proof—that is, God—may only be suppressed at the price of my freedom, my very self. This upward thrust of the human spirit, aspiring always to break free of the mere bone house of its material being, were anyone foolish enough to try and suppress it, would become a great and anguished cry of the heart. "The wild prayer of longing" is how the poet W. H. Auden has called it, against which "all legislation is helpless."

Only the God hypothesis will finally satisfy, because it alone is equal to the hunger and thirst that describe the reach of my mind and heart—the sheer longing of which I find myself entirely possessed—to have perfect peace, happiness, truth, justice, beauty, and goodness. "You would not be looking for me," Christ tells Pascal on that unforgettable night in November 1654 when Jesus suddenly appears before him, speaking those infinitely consoling words, "if you had not already found me." We are all looking for God. Even the atheist is not wholly immune to the germ, the contagion of desire having infected every human being. There is not a sentient being anywhere on the planet who does not wish for deliverance from suffering and death, indeed, who does not long for release from the whole bloody burden of the solitary self.

"What the soul hardly realizes," writes Dom Hubert Van Zeller, a wise and holy Benedictine whom my wife and I were singularly blest to know, "is that, unbeliever or not, his loneliness is really a homesickness for God." The promise, in other words, of sheer unending joy, peace, and all the rest will forever find an echo in the human heart. Lacking this, life would remain unendurable and no person would long remain in it. No one can subsist on a diet of nothing, not even when packaged as a television series.

Who besides the Christian God, in the incomparable gift of his Son, in the kenotic gesture of Christ's love ("costing not less than everything," writes T. S. Eliot), has offered to walk with me through the dark valley, through all the hellishness of sin, sorrow, and loss, in order to accompany me in my final loneliness? "Where no voice can reach us any longer," writes Pope Benedict XVI, "there he is. Hell is thereby overcome, or, to be more accurate, death, which was previously hell, is hell no longer. Neither is the same any longer because there is life in the midst of death, because love dwells in it."

CONCLUSION

I do not think of my brother as often as I used to, in the long years since his death, at age thirty-nine, more than a quarter century ago. None of my children remember him, either because they hadn't yet been born or because, if they had, he was never around to meet them. Living in California, working as an architect between bouts of sickness, he only rarely came home. But then, quite suddenly, in the last months of his life, he came back to say goodbye. He looked pretty awful by then, his broken body ravaged by a killer disease determined to take him down. And by then, of course, it had become painfully obvious to everyone that there was little time left. Still, he seemed cheerful enough, even serene, not wanting to draw attention to himself, and trying to distract us from what the disease was clearly doing to him. It was typical of Kevin to want to shield others from bad news, perhaps to shield himself as well. Even the fact that he had been sick, that his exposure to the HIV infection had been both chronic and acute and was now terminal, were things I certainly did not know until long after the disease had first struck. In fact, it was years before I even cottoned on to the fact of his being gay, a word whose widespread and routine use I continue to resist, especially since there seems so little to characterize as gay in it.

So Kevin died soon after returning to California, fortified, I am told, by the Last Rites of the Church. A piquant detail since he scarcely paid any attention to the Church when he was alive, save only to berate her for her many sins, which mostly had to do with Rome's refusal to sanction the lifestyle he had chosen. But while he had apparently abandoned her, she would never abandon him, thus evincing the attitude of Lot's wife, who, failing to heed the warning about not looking back to witness the destruction of Sodom, is turned into a pillar of salt. The great Irenaeus, bishop and martyr of the early Church, thereupon turns this event to happy account by insisting that here indeed is the perfect image and model of the Church—a mother who cannot turn her back on her own children.

A lovely image. How it endears mother Church to her children!

I suppose, owing to the great differences that marked our attitudes toward the Church, her rigidities regarding the moral law most particularly, one could perhaps characterize our relationship as fairly conflicted, stormy even. And it is true we did cross swords over any number of strictures that, in his mind certainly, old mother Church had no business imposing. In fact, scrubbed down, my brother's position was that for the Church to try and occupy the moral high ground at all was sheer humbuggery; it was all of a piece, he believed, with her overall benightedness, which, by my failing to see it, meant that I too was afflicted with the same sclerosis.

I wish now that I might have avoided some of those minefields, telling him instead things about the Church that, far from setting off incendiary devices in his head, might have helped him to find joy and peace, allowing him to return to the God who remained the real origin and end of his life. Who knows, perhaps less bellicosity on my part might have left him more disposed to accept his moment of grace, moving him closer to that *still point*, where, never mind the screaming incongruities of his life, "past and future / Are conquered and reconciled." Indeed, says T. S. Eliot, reminding us in a stunning Augustinian aside of that realism that finally overcomes the world, "For most of us, this is the aim / Never here to be realized; / Who are only undefeated / Because we have gone on trying."

How I wish, for instance, I'd told him—my now dead brother—about a wonderful book that had just come out, *The Habit of Being*, a superb collection of letters written by Flannery O'Connor, then making its way through an ever-widening circle of admiring readers. He'd have surely loved it, with its bright combination of wit, character, and an insight ideally designed to pierce the hard carapace of a prejudice that had, more and more, become his own habit of being. In one letter, for example, she tells a young woman, a recent convert as it happens, whose exasperation with the Church has already moved her to walk out, "that the Church is the only thing that is going to make the terrible world we are coming to endurable. And that what makes the Church endurable is the fact that she is the Body of Christ and on that Body we are fed."

Bingo. A perfect bull's eye. How consoling is that? Was there ever a tale told that you or I would rather find true? So, yes, I do wish that I had spoken more about Christ to Kevin, had tried to show him Christ, rather than hurling missiles armed with copybook homilies as if faith were a manual of ethics and not a communion with the living God. Had I only drawn my fire less frequently from Torquemada than that of Il Poverello, the universally beloved Francis of Assisi, for whom it was never Christianity that he loved but only Christ, who knows what changes grace might have wrought? He and I were living in Atlanta at the time—I a student at Emory, he working as a waiter—living on the same street, in fact, but in separate apartments, and there were surely moments when I ought to have tried to break through.

A single imperishable memory survives that time of missed opportunity—survives, too, the life of the brother I hardly knew, plus, of course, our mother and father, who are no longer here either. It was Thanksgiving and our parents had come to visit. They stayed a few days, during which we all managed to get along, Kevin and I heroically submerging our differences for the sake of the peace. Yet that isn't what stays in the memory. Rather, I remember a Mass I had gone to that morning, Thanksgiving Day, offered by a young Irish priest, whose words left an impression on me that time will not leave. They changed my life, in fact, resulting in a sort of sea change in the way I view hope. That I see it as the very springboard to eternal life, the fulcrum lifting the world onto the plane of God's glory, is something I owe to words he spoke—and not even his own words, but those of Rainer Maria Rilke, written in a poem called "Autumn," which he read memorably.

> The leaves are falling, falling as
>   from way off,
> as though far gardens withered in
>   the skies;
> they are falling with denying
>   gestures.
> And in the nights the heavy earth is
>   falling
> from all the stars down into
>   loneliness.
> We all are falling. This hand falls.
> And look at others: it is in them all.

And yet there is One who holds
   this falling
endlessly gently in his hands.[12]

This is such a beautiful poem, the rhythm and imagery of the thing as lovely and lapidary as though it had been freshly etched upon the soul. And, really, the words are the most deeply consoling I'd ever heard, spoken with such lucid, lilting insistence on the truth of what Rilke had wanted to say. And what exactly does Rilke intend to say? What is the truth of which his words stand as tokens, as the very imprint of something so profound and ineffaceable as to bring about a sea change in my life? What truth acts as a catalyst, no less, requiring me all at once to reconfigure my entire relationship to hope—indeed, to that "still point of the turning world," toward which the movement of grace would have us all go?

While not wishing to fall into the heresy of paraphrase, and anxious too that I not "murder to dissect," I will nevertheless throw caution to the wind and say that what makes the poem work for me is the tension Rilke sustains throughout between gravity and grace—the two bookends between which all human life moves: the downward pull of the one and the upward surge of the other—and the enticements of Eros versus the enervations of entropy. At one end is the weight of sin, depravity, and death; at the other end is a sudden exhilaration of grace, glory, and God. And you and I are the middle point between the two: a sheer line of horizon betwixt time and eternity, human history and divine mystery. Who is equal to the tension? At once anchored to flesh— bone, marrow, and matter—our souls may at any moment be wafted into purest seraphic space. "The high untrespassed sanctity of space" is how the poet John Gillespie Magee Jr. puts it, when one has at last "slipped the surly bonds of earth, / And danced the skies on laughter-silvered wings."

> And, while with silent lifting mind
>   I've trod
> The high untrespassed sanctity of
>   space,
> Put out my hand, and touched the
>   face of God.[13]

Only Christ can pull off a miracle this sublime. Only he can mediate the difference between the heart that longs for release from death and desolation, and the head that knows there is only the fall into finitude and death. Only Christ, in other words, perfectly qualifies to be that point of intersection, the *still point*, where time and eternity, nature and grace, God and man all suddenly come together, annealed in the Body and the Blood of a humanity assumed by God himself. The *still point*, says Dante in the *Paradiso*, is "where every where and every when is focused."

Jesus Christ, then, is the bridge, the only bridge we've got, over the sea of this fallen and finite world, shepherding us into the arms of an infinite God who freely chooses to love us forever. "Let him easter in us," implores Gerard Manley Hopkins in "The Wreck of the Deutschland," a poem that no one would publish in his own lifetime, but which has become a monument to his genius in the century following his death. Let Christ, he says, "be a dayspring to the dimness of us, be a / crimson-cresseted east." Let us, in other words, become like the tall, gaunt nun found at the center of the ship's drama, who, in the final moments of her life, is heard repeatedly crying out, "*O Christ, Christ, come quickly.*"

As the great St. Irenaeus reminds us, "He (Christ) raises man from the ground to which he has fallen, and by giving the whole of man scope in himself, he also assumes man's death into himself." Yes, we all are falling, the germ of death has insinuated its poison deep within us all; but if we look to Christ, "who holds this falling / endlessly gently in his hands," we needn't be afraid.

Isn't the hope and the desire that all this be true—indeed, that it must be so else there can be no way to explain so deep and persisting a need—does it not find an answering response in the gift, the unforeseeable gift, in which God himself offers to accompany me every step of the way, indeed, all the way to him who dwells in that otherwise unapproachable light, happiness, and peace we call heaven?

> For Christ plays in ten thousand
>   places,
> Lovely in limbs, and lovely in eyes
>   not his
> To the Father through the features
>   of men's faces.[14]

None of us need be fearful of the mess we're in; we mustn't despair of the story we find ourselves stuck in just because the details appear bleak and unredeeming. It is not a narrative going nowhere; we've not fallen into a Jean Paul Sartre drama called *No Exit*, in which hell is other people. The fact is, we know the outcome of the story; our faith tells us. And so in hope we are free to move in the direction of the final act, which ends on a note of triumphant, unending love. Because, at the end of the day, each of us is known to God by name, a name he speaks with delight from the very depths of his heart, whose vibrations even now I pray my mother, my brother, and my father rejoice to feel.

> *"Who am I, Lord, that You should know my name?"*

NOTES

1. Excerpted from T. S. Eliot, *The Four Quartets* (New York: Houghton Mifflin Harcourt Books, 1968).

2. Excerpted from Emily Dickinson and Thomas Herbert Johnson, *Complete Poems of Emily Dickenson* (Mattituck, NY: Ameron LTD, 1976).

3. Excerpted from Alfred Tennyson, *The Collected Works of Alfred Tennyson* (New York: Oxford University Press, 2009).

4. Excerpted from Gerard Manley Hopkins, "Terrible Sonnets" in *The Collected Works of Gerard Manley Hopkins* (New York: Oxford University Press, 2006).

5. Excerpted from Richard Wilbur, "The House" in *Anterooms: New Poems and Translation* (New York: Houghton Mifflin Harcourt Books, 2010).

6. Excerpted from T. S. Eliot, *The Four Quartets* (New York: Houghton Mifflin Harcourt Books, 1968).

7. Excerpted from William Shakespeare, "Measure for Measure" in *First Folio* (Philadelphia: Henry T. Coates, 1859).

8. Excerpted from Henry King, "The Exequy" in *The Poems of Bishop Henry King* (Folcroft, PA: Folcroft Library Editions, 1973).

9. Excerpted from Edna St. Vincent Millay, "Dirge Without Music" in *Collected Sonnets of Edna St. Vincent Millay* (New York: Harper and Brothers, 1941).

10. Excerpted from John Gillespie Magee Jr., "Sunward I've Climbed" in Hermann Hagedorn, *Sunward I've Climbed: The Story of John Magee, poet and soldier, 1922-1941* (New York: The Macmillan Company, 1942).

11. Excerpted from Gerard Manley Hopkins, *The Collected Works of Gerard Manley Hopkins* (New York: Oxford University Press, 2006).

Regis Martin is a professor of theology at Franciscan University in Steubenville, Ohio, where he has taught for more than twenty years. He studied in Rome at the Angelicum, graduating summa cum laude in 1988 with a doctorate in sacred theology. Martin is the author of a half-dozen books and specializes in courses on the Trinity, Christology, Church, grace, sacraments, the writings of Hans Urs von Balthasar, and the Catholic Literary Revival. Married and living in Steubenville, he is the father of ten children and has five grandchildren.

Founded in 1865, Ave Maria Press,
a ministry of the Congregation of
Holy Cross, is a Catholic publishing
company that serves the spiritual and
formative needs of the Church and its
schools, institutions, and ministers;
Christian individuals and families; and
others seeking spiritual nourishment.

For a complete listing of.titles from

Ave Maria Press

Sorin Books

Forest of Peace

Christian Classics

visit www.avemariapress.com

ave maria press® / Notre Dame, IN 46556
A Ministry of the United States Province of Holy Cross